ABSTRACT

This unit plan outlines a dynamic approach to teaching economics and personal finance through gamification techniques. Designed for high school students, the unit spans four weeks and integrates fundamental economic principles with practical financial literacy concepts. Through interactive activities, group discussions, and adapted games inspired by "The Price is Right," students

Contents

Digital Copy 3
Unit Plan: Gamifying Economics and Personal Finance 4
Lesson Plans 7
Day 1 Lesson Plan: Introduction to Economics 7
    Handout A: 9
    Handout B: 11
Day 2 Lesson Plan: Market Structures 12
Day 3 Lesson Plan: Price Determination 16
    Handout D: 18
    Handout E: 19
Day 4 Lesson Plan: Introduction to Personal Finance 21
    Handout F: 23
    Handout G: 26
Day 5 Lesson Plan: Budgeting Basics 29
    Handout H: 31
    Handout I: 33
    Handout J: 35
Day 6 Lesson Plan: Saving and Investing 37
    Handout K 39
    Handout L 42
    Handout M 46
Day 7 Lesson Plan: Incorporating "The Price is Right" Games 48
    Handout N 50
Day 8 Lesson Plan: Plinko Budgeting Challenge 52
    Handout O 54
Day 9 Lesson Plan: Spin the Wheel of Investments 56
   Wheel Setup 58
    Handout P 59
    Handout Q 60
Day 10 Lesson Plan: Tackling Real-World Financial Decisions 61
   Presentation Rubric 64
   Example Scenarios 65

Handout R 67
Day 11 Lesson Plan: Putting It All Together: Your Financial Masterplan 70
　　Sample Rubric 72
　　Handout S 73
Day 12 Lesson Plan: Gamification & Your Future Finances 76
　　Handout T 78
　　The Price is Econ Completion Award 0

Digital Copy

By purchasing this title, you may request a digital copy of the handouts contained within, please email me at jeremiah@bullfroglearning.net

Thank you for your support!

Unit Plan: Gamifying Economics and Personal Finance

Unit Title: Gamifying Economics and Personal Finance

Grade Level: High School

Duration: 4 weeks

Objectives:

- Students will demonstrate an understanding of basic economic principles and personal finance concepts.
- Students will apply critical thinking skills to analyze financial decisions and their consequences.
- Students will develop budgeting, saving, and investing strategies through interactive games and activities.

Week 1: Introduction to Economic Principles

- **Day 1:** Introduction to Economics
    - Define economics and its branches (microeconomics and macroeconomics).
    - Discuss fundamental economic concepts such as scarcity, opportunity cost, and supply and demand.
    - Group activity: Scarcity simulation game where students experience limited resources and must make choices.
- **Day 2:** Market Structures
    - Introduce different types of market structures (perfect competition, monopoly, oligopoly, monopolistic competition).
    - Group discussion: Analyze real-world examples of companies and their market structures.
    - Class debate: Pros and cons of different market structures.
- **Day 3:** Price Determination
    - Explain how prices are determined in markets through the interaction of supply and demand.
    - Graphical analysis: Demand and supply curves, equilibrium price, and quantity.
    - Group activity: Price negotiation simulation game.

Week 2: Personal Finance Fundamentals

- **Day 4:** Introduction to Personal Finance
    - Define personal finance and its importance.

- Discuss key personal finance concepts such as budgeting, saving, investing, and managing debt.
- Group activity: Personal finance quiz game to assess prior knowledge.
- **Day 5:** Budgeting Basics
    - Explain the importance of budgeting and how to create a budget.
    - Interactive budgeting activity: Students create personal budgets based on different income scenarios.
    - Review common budgeting pitfalls and strategies to overcome them.
- **Day 6:** Saving and Investing
    - Discuss the difference between saving and investing.
    - Introduce basic investment options (e.g., stocks, bonds, mutual funds).
    - Group activity: Investment simulation game (e.g., stock market game) where students invest virtual money and track their portfolio performance.

Week 3: Games Integration

- **Day 7:** Incorporating "The Price is Right" Games
    - Introduce "The Price is Right" games and their connection to economics and personal finance concepts.
    - Analyze video clips from the show to identify economic principles at play.
- **Day 8:** Game Adaptation: Plinko Budgeting
    - Explain the rules of Plinko and how it will be adapted to teach budgeting.
    - Students participate in the Plinko budgeting game, distributing funds to different spending categories based on where the disc lands.
- **Day 9:** Game Adaptation: Spin the Wheel Investment
    - Adapt the "Spin the Wheel" game to teach investment principles.
    - Students spin a wheel to determine investment returns and discuss risk-reward trade-offs.

Week 4: Application and Review

- **Day 10:** Application of Concepts
    - Students apply economic and personal finance concepts learned throughout the unit to real-world scenarios.
    - Group presentations: Students present their analyses and recommendations for financial decisions.

- **Day 11:** Review and Assessment
    - Review key concepts covered in the unit.
    - Assessment: Individual or group project where students create a comprehensive financial plan based on a given scenario.
- **Day 12:** Reflection and Wrap-Up
    - Reflect on the unit's objectives and learning outcomes.
    - Class discussion: What have students learned about economics and personal finance through gamification?
    - Wrap-up activity: Personal finance pledge where students commit to implementing what they've learned in their own financial lives.

Assessment:

- Participation in class discussions and activities.
- Completion of individual and group assignments.
- Performance in game-based assessments.
- Reflection on personal finance goals and strategies.

Materials:

- Whiteboard and markers
- Scarcity simulation materials (e.g., tokens representing resources)
- Graph paper and markers for graphical analysis
- Budgeting worksheets
- Stock market simulation software or online platforms
- Materials for adapted "The Price is Right" games (e.g., Plinko board, wheel spinner)

Conclusion: By gamifying economics and personal finance concepts, students will not only gain a deeper understanding of these topics but also develop practical skills that they can apply in their own lives. Through interactive games and activities, students will learn to make informed financial decisions and navigate the complexities of the modern economy.

Lesson Plans

Day 1 Lesson Plan: Introduction to Economics

Objective: Students will understand the fundamental concepts of economics, including scarcity, opportunity cost, and supply and demand.

Materials Needed:

1. Whiteboard and markers
2. Scarcity simulation materials (e.g., tokens, paper cutouts representing resources)
    1. Handout A: Simulation Worksheet
    2. Handout B: Unexpected Event Cards
3. Handout: Key Terms and Definitions
4. PowerPoint slides or visual aids (optional)

Duration: 60 minutes

Procedure:

Introduction (5 minutes):

1. Welcome students to the first lesson of the unit on economics.
2. Explain the importance of understanding economics in making informed decisions in both personal and professional life.
3. Preview the objectives of the lesson.

Engagement (10 minutes):

1. Ask students to brainstorm examples of situations where they have experienced scarcity (e.g., limited time, money, or resources).
2. Discuss their responses and define scarcity as the condition of having limited resources compared to unlimited wants and needs.
3. Introduce the concept of opportunity cost as the value of the next best alternative forgone when a decision is made.

Instruction (20 minutes):

1. Present a brief lecture or use PowerPoint slides to explain the following concepts:
    - Scarcity: Definition and examples
    - Opportunity Cost: Definition and importance in decision-making

- Production Possibility Frontier (PPF): Introduce the concept and demonstrate how it illustrates the trade-offs between two goods or services.

2. Use real-world examples to illustrate these concepts (e.g., choosing between studying for a test or going out with friends).
3. Provide opportunities for students to ask questions and clarify any misunderstandings.

Activity - Scarcity Simulation (20 minutes):

1. Divide the class into small groups.
2. Distribute scarcity simulation materials (tokens or paper cutouts representing resources).
3. Explain the rules of the simulation:
   - Each group has a set of resources (tokens).
   - Each round represents a decision-making period where groups must allocate their resources to different needs or wants (e.g., food, shelter, education).
   - Groups must prioritize their allocations based on their preferences and needs.
4. Conduct several rounds of the simulation, gradually increasing the complexity by introducing new factors (e.g., unexpected events, changes in available resources).
5. After each round, facilitate a discussion on the choices made by each group, the trade-offs they faced, and the concept of opportunity cost.

Conclusion (5 minutes):

1. Review the key concepts covered in the lesson: scarcity, opportunity cost, and decision-making.
2. Distribute the handout with key terms and definitions for students to review.
3. Preview the topics to be covered in the next lesson.

Homework/Extension: Assign students to write a reflection on how the concepts of scarcity and opportunity cost apply to their daily lives. Encourage them to provide specific examples and analyze the trade-offs they encounter in decision-making.

Assessment: Monitor students' participation in the scarcity simulation activity and their understanding of the concepts discussed during class discussions. Collect and review students' reflections for deeper comprehension.

Note: Adjust the complexity of the concepts and activities based on the students' prior knowledge and grade level. Provide additional support or scaffolding for struggling students as needed.

Handout A:
Scarcity Simulation Worksheet

Instructions: You are about to participate in a simulation activity to understand the concept of scarcity and its implications for decision-making. Follow the instructions carefully and work with your group to make decisions in each round.

Round 1: Allocation of Resources

1. You are given 10 tokens, representing your available resources.
2. As a group, discuss and decide how to allocate your resources among the following needs or wants:
    - Food
    - Shelter
    - Education
    - Entertainment
3. Write down your allocation for each category in the table below.

Category	Tokens Allocated
Food	
Shelter	
Education	
Entertainment	

Round 2: Unexpected Events

1. Each group will receive a random event card that affects their available resources.
2. Discuss and decide how to adjust your allocations based on the new circumstances.
3. Write down your adjusted allocations in the table below.

Category	Tokens Allocated
Food	
Shelter	
Education	
Entertainment	

Round 3: Changing Priorities

1. The availability of resources has changed, and you now have only 5 tokens to allocate.
2. Reevaluate your group's priorities and decide on a new allocation strategy.
3. Write down your updated allocations in the table below.

Category	Tokens Allocated
Food	
Shelter	
Education	
Entertainment	

Reflection Questions:
1. How did your group approach decision-making in each round?
2. What trade-offs did you have to make when allocating resources?
3. How did unexpected events and changes in resource availability affect your decisions?
4. What did you learn about the concept of scarcity from this activity?
5. How can you apply the concepts of scarcity and opportunity cost to real-life situations?

Instructions for Reflection: Discuss the reflection questions with your group members and write down your responses. Be prepared to share your insights with the class during the debriefing session.

Handout B:

Natural Disaster: A severe storm has damaged your group's shelter, requiring additional resources for repairs. **Lose 3 resource tokens for shelter repair.**	**Medical Emergency:** One member of your group has fallen ill and needs medical treatment, reducing the group's available resources. **Lose 2 resource tokens for medical treatment.**
Job Loss: One member of your group has lost their job, leading to a decrease in income and available resources. **Lose 4 resource tokens due to decreased income.**	**Price Increase:** The cost of food has unexpectedly risen, putting pressure on your group's budget for essential needs **Lose 2 resource tokens due to increased food costs.**
Windfall: Your group has received an unexpected windfall of resources (e.g., winning a contest), providing a temporary boost to your available resources. **Gain 5 extra resource tokens.**	**Opportunity for Extra Income:** One member of your group can take on an extra job, increasing the group's income and available resources. **Gain 3 extra resource tokens.**
Family Emergency: Another member of your group needs to travel urgently to attend to a family emergency, requiring additional resources for transportation and support. **Lose 3 resource tokens for emergency travel expenses.**	**Equipment Breakdown:** The group's essential equipment (e.g., stove, computer) has malfunctioned and needs repair or replacement, reducing available resources. **Lose 2 resource tokens for equipment repair or replacement.**
Unexpected Bill: Your group has received an unexpected bill (e.g., medical bill, repair bill) that requires immediate payment, impacting your available resources. **Lose 3 resource tokens for bill payment.**	**Community Donation:** Your group has received a donation from the community (e.g., food drive, clothing donation), providing extra resources for your needs. **Gain 4 extra resource tokens.**

Day 2 Lesson Plan: Market Structures

Grade Level: High School

Subject: Economics

Duration: 60 minutes

Objective:

- Students will understand the characteristics of different market structures.
- Students will analyze real-world examples to identify market structures.
- Students will engage in a class debate to discuss the advantages and disadvantages of various market structures.

Materials:

- Whiteboard and markers
- Handouts with definitions of different market structures
- Real-world examples of companies and industries (e.g., tech industry, fast-food chains)
- Debate guidelines and rubric

Warm-Up (5 minutes):

- Begin the lesson by asking students to recall the concept of supply and demand from the previous lesson.
- Review the basics of supply and demand briefly and ask students to consider how supply and demand interact in different types of markets.

Introduction to Market Structures (10 minutes):

1. Define market structures: Perfect competition, monopoly, oligopoly, monopolistic competition.
2. Explain the characteristics of each market structure using examples and visual aids.
3. Emphasize key differences in terms of number of firms, product differentiation, barriers to entry, and control over prices.
4. Ask students to take notes on the characteristics of each market structure.

Activity: Analyzing Real-World Examples (20 minutes):

1. Divide students into small groups.
2. Distribute handouts with real-world examples of companies and industries.
3. Instruct each group to analyze their assigned example and identify the market structure that best describes it.

4. Encourage students to consider factors such as the number of competitors, product differentiation, and barriers to entry.
5. Allow time for groups to discuss and prepare their findings.

Group Presentations (15 minutes):

1. Invite each group to present their analysis to the class.
2. After each presentation, facilitate a brief discussion to compare the market structures identified by different groups.
3. Encourage students to ask questions and provide feedback on each other's analyses.

Class Debate: Pros and Cons of Market Structures (10 minutes):

1. Divide the class into two groups: one group representing the advantages of competitive markets and the other group representing the advantages of monopoly markets.
2. Provide each group with a list of arguments to support their assigned position.
3. Allow time for groups to prepare their arguments.
4. Conduct the debate, with each group presenting their arguments and responding to counterarguments from the opposing group.
5. Encourage respectful and constructive discussion among students.

Conclusion and Reflection (5 minutes):

- Summarize the key points discussed during the lesson.
- Ask students to reflect on what they have learned about market structures and how they apply to real-world businesses and industries.
- Assign homework if necessary, such as reading on market structures or preparing for the next lesson.

Extension Activity (Optional):

- Assign a writing task where students analyze a specific industry and evaluate its market structure's impact on consumers, producers, and society.
- Encourage students to use evidence from class discussions and research to support their arguments.

Assessment:

- Participation in group activities and discussions.
- Accuracy of analysis in identifying market structures for real-world examples.
- Quality of arguments presented during the debate.
- Completion of reflection activity demonstrating understanding of key concepts.

Note: Ensure that the debate is well-moderated to maintain a respectful and inclusive learning environment. Provide guidance and support to students who may struggle with understanding complex economic concepts.

Handout C:

Perfect Competition:
• Article: "Why Farmers' Markets Are the Perfect Example of Perfect Competition"
    • Summary: This article explores how farmers' markets operate as examples of perfect competition. It discusses the large number of small-scale producers selling homogeneous products, the ease of entry and exit into the market, and the lack of market power among individual sellers.
• Source: The Balance Small Business
	Monopoly:
	• Article: "The Rise and Reign of Amazon: Understanding Monopolistic Power in E-Commerce"
	    • Summary: This article analyzes Amazon's dominance in the e-commerce industry, highlighting its control over most online retail sales and the barriers to entry for potential competitors. It discusses the implications of Amazon's monopoly power on consumer choice and market competition.
	• Source: Forbes

Oligopoly:
• Article: "The Smartphone Wars: Oligopoly Dynamics in the Mobile Industry"
    • Summary: This article examines the oligopolistic nature of the mobile phone industry, focusing on the competition among a small number of major players such as Apple, Samsung, and Huawei. It discusses how these companies compete for market share through product differentiation, pricing strategies, and innovation.
• Source: Investopedia
	Monopolistic Competition:
	• Article: "Fast Fashion and Monopolistic Competition: The Case of Zara"
	    • Summary: This article explores Zara's business model in the fast-fashion industry as an example of monopolistic competition. It discusses Zara's emphasis on product differentiation, rapid inventory turnover, and pricing strategies to distinguish itself from competitors while still operating in a crowded market.
	• Source: Business Insider

Natural Monopoly:
• Article: "Understanding Natural Monopolies: The Case of Utility Companies"
    • Summary: This article explains the concept of natural monopolies using utility companies (e.g., water, electricity) as examples. It discusses the high fixed costs associated with infrastructure development and the economies of scale that make it more efficient for a single firm to provide these essential services in each geographic area.
• Source: The Balance
	Regulated Monopoly:
	• Article: "The Role of Regulated Monopolies in Telecommunications"
	    • Summary: This article examines the role of regulated monopolies in the telecommunications industry, focusing on companies like AT&T and Verizon in the United States. It discusses how government regulations aim to balance the need for competition with the necessity of providing essential services to consumers.
	• Source: Federal Communications Commission (FCC)

Day 3 Lesson Plan: Price Determination

Objective: Students will understand how prices are determined in markets through the interaction of supply and demand.

Materials Needed:

- Whiteboard and markers
- Graph paper and markers
- Handouts with scenarios for price negotiation simulation game

Introduction (10 minutes):

1. Review key concepts from previous lessons, such as scarcity, opportunity cost, and supply and demand.
2. Explain that today's focus will be on understanding how prices are determined in markets.

Activity 1: Graphical Analysis (20 minutes):

1. Review the basics of demand and supply curves on the whiteboard.
2. Draw a demand curve and a supply curve on the whiteboard, labeling the axes and equilibrium point.
3. Explain how changes in demand and supply affect equilibrium price and quantity.
4. Engage students in a discussion about factors that can shift demand and supply curves (e.g., changes in consumer preferences, technology, input prices).
5. Provide examples and ask students to predict the impact on equilibrium price and quantity.

Activity 2: Price Negotiation Simulation Game (30 minutes):

1. Divide the class into pairs or small groups.
2. Distribute handouts with scenarios for a price negotiation simulation game. Each scenario should include details about a buyer and a seller negotiating a price for a product or service.
3. Instruct students to take on the roles of the buyer and seller and negotiate a price based on their perceived value and willingness to pay/sell.
4. Circulate the room to observe the negotiations and provide guidance as needed.
5. After negotiations are complete, reconvene as a class to debrief.
6. Discuss the outcomes of the negotiations and how they relate to the concepts of supply, demand, and equilibrium price.
7. Facilitate a discussion about strategies for successful negotiation and the role of bargaining power in determining prices.

Conclusion (10 minutes):

1. Summarize the key takeaways from the lesson.
2. Connect the activities to real-world examples of price determination.
3. Encourage students to reflect on how understanding supply and demand dynamics can help them make informed decisions as consumers and producers.

Homework/Extension Activity:

- Assign students to find examples of price changes in the news or in their own experiences and analyze the factors influencing those changes.

Assessment:

- Participation in class discussions and activities.
- Observation of students' engagement and understanding during the negotiation simulation game.
- Informal assessment through questioning during the lesson.

Note: Adjust the duration of activities based on class pace and student engagement. Be prepared to provide additional explanation or examples as needed to ensure understanding.

Handout D:

Instructions:

1. Study the examples provided below.
2. Use the graph paper to draw demand and supply curves for each scenario.
3. Label the axes appropriately and indicate the equilibrium price and quantity.
4. Analyze the impact of changes in demand or supply on the equilibrium price and quantity.

Example 1: Scenario: The market for smartphones

- Initially, the demand for smartphones increases due to the release of a highly anticipated new model.
- At the same time, the cost of production decreases due to advancements in technology.

Example 2: Scenario: The market for coffee

- A severe frost in coffee-producing regions reduces the supply of coffee beans.
- Consumer tastes shift towards specialty coffee drinks, increasing demand for premium coffee beans.

Example 3: Scenario: The market for rental apartments

- Many new apartment buildings are being constructed, increasing the rental unit supply.
- Job growth in the area leads to an influx of new residents, increasing demand for rental housing.

Example 4: Scenario: The market for used cars

- Rising fuel prices cause consumers to demand more fuel-efficient vehicles, decreasing demand for gas-guzzling SUVs.
- A shortage of semiconductor chips disrupts the production of new cars, reducing the supply of both new and used vehicles.

Questions:

1. For each example, describe the initial impact of the change in demand or supply on equilibrium price and quantity.
2. How might producers and consumers respond to these changes in the long run?
3. Provide real-world examples of similar supply and demand shocks that have affected markets you are familiar with.

Handout E:
Worksheet: Price Negotiation Simulation Game

Objective: To practice negotiation skills and understand how bargaining power influences prices in a market.

Instructions:

1. Read the scenario provided below carefully.
2. Decide whether you will take on the role of the buyer or the seller.
3. Use the negotiation tips discussed in class to strategize your approach.
4. Work with your partner to negotiate a price for the product or service in the scenario.
5. Record the final agreed-upon price and any additional terms reached during the negotiation.

Scenario:

You are either a buyer or a seller in the following scenarios. Choose your role based on your preference and begin the negotiation process with your partner.

1. **Scenario 1:**
    - Product/Service: Used textbook for a college course
    - Buyer: You are a student looking to buy a used textbook for your upcoming course.
    - Seller: You are a student who has completed the course and wants to sell your used textbook.

2. **Scenario 2:**
    - Product/Service: Handmade jewelry
    - Buyer: You are looking for a unique gift for a friend and are interested in purchasing handmade jewelry.
    - Seller: You are an artisan who creates and sells handmade jewelry at local craft fairs.

3. **Scenario 3:**
    - Product/Service: Graphic design services for a logo
    - Buyer: You are a small business owner in need of a professional logo for your company.
    - Seller: You are a freelance graphic designer with experience creating logos for businesses.

Negotiation Tips:

- Know your priorities and walk-away points.
- Listen actively and ask clarifying questions.

- Be prepared to compromise and find mutually beneficial solutions.
- Use persuasive language and provide rationale for your offers.

Negotiation Record:

Scenario	Role (Buyer/Seller)	Initial Offer	Counteroffer(s)	Final Price
Scenario 1				
Scenario 2				
Scenario 3				

Reflection Questions:

1. What negotiation strategies did you find most effective during the simulation game?
2. How did your role (buyer or seller) influence your negotiation approach?
3. What factors do you think influenced the final agreed-upon price in each scenario?
4. How does this negotiation experience relate to real-world buying and selling situations?

Conclusion: Reflect on the negotiation process and consider how understanding bargaining power and effective communication can lead to successful outcomes in business transactions. Apply the skills learned in this simulation game to future negotiations in your personal and professional life.

Day 4 Lesson Plan: Introduction to Personal Finance

Objective: Students will demonstrate prior knowledge of personal finance concepts and will be introduced to key concepts such as budgeting, saving, and investing.

Materials Needed:

- Whiteboard and markers
- Handouts: Personal finance pre-assessment quiz
- Examples of budget templates
- Personal finance resources (books, websites, etc.)

Introduction (10 minutes):

1. Welcome students to Day Four of the unit on economics and personal finance.
2. Review the lesson's objectives: to assess prior knowledge of personal finance concepts and introduce key financial principles.
3. Discuss the importance of personal finance in individuals' lives and why it's essential to learn about managing money effectively.

Activity 1: Personal Finance Pre-Assessment Quiz (20 minutes):

1. Distribute the personal finance pre-assessment quiz to each student.
2. Instruct students to complete the quiz individually.
3. The quiz should cover basic personal finance concepts such as budgeting, saving, investing, and managing debt.
4. After completing the quiz, collect the papers and review them to identify common areas of strength and weakness.

Activity 2: Introduction to Key Personal Finance Concepts (30 minutes):

1. Based on the results of the pre-assessment quiz, identify key concepts that students need further instruction on.
2. Begin by defining budgeting and its importance in personal finance.
3. Discuss the components of a budget: income, expenses, savings, and discretionary spending.
4. Show examples of different budget templates or worksheets.
5. Explain how to create a basic budget, including estimating income and tracking expenses.
6. Briefly introduce the concepts of saving and investing, emphasizing their importance in building wealth over time.
7. Provide examples of different savings and investment vehicles (e.g., savings accounts, stocks, bonds).

8. Discuss the importance of managing debt responsibly and briefly introduce strategies for debt management.

Conclusion (10 minutes):

1. Summarize the key concepts covered in the lesson: budgeting, saving, investing, and managing debt.

2. Emphasize the importance of these concepts in achieving financial stability and long-term goals.

3. Encourage students to reflect on their personal finance habits and consider areas for improvement.

4. Provide additional resources for further learning, such as personal finance books or websites.

Homework/Extension (Optional): Assign students to create a simple budget for themselves based on their current income and expenses. They can bring their budgets to the next class for discussion and feedback.

Assessment:

- Completion and accuracy of the personal finance pre-assessment quiz.

- Participation in class discussions and engagement with key concepts.

- The quality of students' understanding is demonstrated in their contributions to class activities and discussions.

Handout F:

Pre-Assessment Quiz: Personal Finance

Multiple Choice:

1. What is the purpose of budgeting?

    A. To spend money impulsively

    B. To track income and expenses

    C. To accumulate debt

    D. To ignore financial goals

2. Which of the following is considered a fixed expense?

    A. Groceries

    B. Rent or mortgage

    C. Entertainment

    D. Dining out

3. Which of the following is an example of an investment?

    A. Buying a car

    B. Purchasing stocks

    C. Paying off credit card debt

    D. Renting an apartment

4. What does ROI stand for in the context of personal finance?

    A. Return on investment

    B. Rent or income

    C. Rate of inflation

    D. Real estate opportunity index

5. Which of the following is typically true regarding savings accounts and certificates of deposit (CDs)?

    A. Savings accounts typically offer higher interest rates than CDs.

    B. CDs typically offer higher interest rates than savings accounts.

    C. Both savings accounts and CDs offer similar interest rates.

    D. Savings accounts and CDs do not earn interest.

6. Which of the following is NOT a common type of retirement account?

    A. 401(k)

    B. IRA (Individual Retirement Account)

    C. HSA (Health Savings Account)

    D. Roth IRA

7. What should be prioritized before saving for emergencies?

    A. Investing in the stock market

    B. Paying off high-interest debt

    C. Purchasing luxury items

    D. Taking expensive vacations

8. What is the term for the money owed to lenders?

    A. Assets

    B. Liabilities

    C. Equity

    D. Revenue

9. Which of the following is an example of a variable expense?

    A. Rent

    B. Utilities

    C. Car payment

    D. Insurance premiums

10. What is the purpose of an emergency fund?

    A. To finance vacations

    B. To cover unexpected expenses

    C. To invest in the stock market

    D. To pay off debt quickly

True/False: Indicate whether each statement is true or false.

11. Investing in stocks is risk-free.

12. Compound interest means earning interest on the initial principal only.

13. A Roth IRA allows tax-free withdrawals in retirement.

14. An increase in the Federal Reserve's interest rates typically leads to lower mortgage rates.

15. A credit score of 800 or above is considered poor.

Matching: Match each term with its corresponding definition.

Term	Definition
16. Assets	A. Money borrowed from a bank
17. Compound interest	B. Resources owned by an individual
18. Credit card	C. Interest calculated on the initial principal and on the accumulated interest
19. Net worth	D. Plastic card issued by financial institutions allowing the cardholder to borrow funds
20. Mortgage	E. Total assets minus total liabilities

Fill in the Blank:

21. A _____ is a detailed plan for managing money.

22. The process of spreading out investments to reduce risk is called _____.

23. A _____ is a loan specifically for purchasing a home.

24. _____ is the process of paying off debt over time with regular payments.

Short Essay Question: Explain the importance of saving and investing for long-term financial goals, providing at least two examples of financial goals and how saving and investing can help achieve them.

Handout G:
Activity 2: Introduction to Key Personal Finance Concepts

I. Introduction to Key Concepts

A. Definition of Budgeting

    1. Importance in personal finance

    2. Components of a budget

II. Budgeting Basics

A. Components of a Budget

    1. Income

    2. Expenses

    3. Savings

    4. Discretionary Spending

III. Introduction to Saving and Investing

A. Difference between Saving and Investing

    1. Saving

    2. Investing

B. Importance of Saving and Investing

C. Examples of Investment Vehicles

    1. Savings Accounts

        1. Savings Accounts

        2. Money Market

        3. Certificate of Deposit

    2. Stocks

    3. Bonds

IV. Credit and Insurance

A. Understanding Credit

    1. Definition of credit

    2. Importance of credit history

B. Strategies for Managing Debt

    1. Importance of responsible debt management

    2. Strategies for paying off debt

    3. Factors affecting credit score

C. Types of Insurance

1. Health insurance
    I. HMO
    II. PPO

2. Auto insurance
    I. Comprehensive
    II. Collision
    III. Liability

3. Homeowners or renters' insurance

4. Life insurance
    I. Whole Life
    II. Term Life

5. 5. Importance of insurance coverage

Day 5 Lesson Plan: Budgeting Basics

Objective: Students will understand the importance of budgeting and learn how to create a basic budget.

Materials Needed:

1. Whiteboard and markers
2. Budgeting worksheets or templates
3. Handout: Budgeting Basics Guide
4. Examples of budgeting tools or apps (optional)
5. Projector for PowerPoint slides or visual aids (optional)

Duration: 60 minutes

Procedure:

Introduction (5 minutes):

1. Welcome students to the second lesson of the unit on economics and personal finance.
2. Recap the concepts of scarcity, opportunity cost, and decision-making covered in the previous lesson.
3. Preview the objectives of the current lesson.

Engagement (10 minutes):

1. Ask students to share their thoughts on budgeting. What do they think budgeting means? Why is it important?
2. Facilitate a brief discussion, encouraging students to share their own experiences with budgeting (if any).
3. Introduce the importance of budgeting in managing personal finances and making informed financial decisions.

Instruction (20 minutes):

1. Present a lecture or use PowerPoint slides to explain the following key concepts:
    - Definition of a budget: A financial plan that outlines income and expenses over a specific period.
    - Benefits of budgeting: Helps track spending, prioritize expenses, and achieve financial goals.
    - Components of a budget: Income, fixed expenses, variable expenses, and savings.
2. Discuss different budgeting methods (e.g., zero-based budgeting, 50/30/20 rule) and when each method might be appropriate.

3. Provide examples of common fixed expenses (e.g., rent, utilities) and variable expenses (e.g., groceries, entertainment).
4. Introduce budgeting tools or apps that students can use to create and manage their budgets (if applicable).

Activity - Budgeting Exercise (25 minutes):

1. Distribute budgeting worksheets or templates to each student.
2. Explain the instructions for the budgeting exercise:
    - Students will create a monthly budget based on a given scenario (e.g., a college student with part-time income).
    - They should allocate their income to cover fixed expenses, variable expenses, and savings goals.
3. Allow time for students to work individually or in pairs to complete their budgets.
4. Circulate around the room to provide guidance and answer any questions.
5. After completing the budget, encourage students to reflect on their choices and adjust if necessary.

Conclusion (5 minutes):

1. Review the key concepts covered in the lesson: budgeting, fixed expenses, variable expenses, and savings.
2. Distribute the handout with budgeting tips and resources for students to reference.
3. Summarize the importance of budgeting in achieving financial stability and reaching long-term financial goals.

Homework/Extension: Assign students to track their expenses for one week and compare their actual spending to their budgeted amounts. They can reflect on any discrepancies and identify areas for improvement in their budgeting skills.

Assessment: Evaluate students' understanding of budgeting concepts through their participation in the budgeting exercise and their ability to apply budgeting principles to real-life scenarios. Review completed budgeting worksheets for accuracy and thoroughness.

Note: Adjust the complexity of the budgeting exercise and examples based on the students' grade level and prior knowledge. Provide additional support or resources for students who may need assistance with budgeting concepts.

Handout H:

Scenario: You are a college student with a part-time job earning $800 per month after taxes. You need to create a monthly budget to manage your expenses and savings goals.

Instructions:

1. Use the information provided to allocate your income to cover fixed expenses, variable expenses, and savings goals.
2. Fill in the blanks with your budgeted amounts for each category.
3. Calculate the total of your budgeted expenses and compare it to your monthly income to ensure you are living within your means.
4. After completing your budget, reflect on your choices and adjust if necessary.

Income: Monthly Income: $800

Fixed Expenses:

1. Rent: _____
2. Utilities (electricity, water, etc.): _____
3. Internet/Cable: _____
4. Phone Bill: _____
5. Transportation (bus pass, gas, etc.): _____
6. Insurance (health, car, etc.): _____

Variable Expenses:

1. Groceries/Food: _____
2. Dining Out/Entertainment: _____
3. Clothing/Personal Care: _____
4. Transportation (additional expenses): _____
5. School Supplies/Books: _____
6. Miscellaneous (e.g., hobbies, gifts): _____

Savings Goals:

1. Emergency Fund: _____
2. College Tuition/Savings: _____
3. Other Savings Goals (e.g., travel, future purchases): _____

Reflection:

1. Are there any categories where you had to make trade-offs or sacrifices? Explain.
2. Did you allocate enough for your savings goals? If not, how can you adjust your budget to prioritize savings?
3. What challenges did you encounter while creating your budget, and how did you overcome them?
4. What strategies will you use to stick to your budget and track your expenses?

Instructions for Reflection: Reflect on your budgeting decisions and answer the reflection questions provided. Consider how you can improve your budgeting skills and achieve your financial goals effectively.

Handout I:
50-30-20 Budgeting Exercise Worksheet

Scenario: You are a recent college graduate starting your first full-time job with a monthly income of $3,000 after taxes. You have heard about the 50-30-20 budgeting rule and want to use it to manage your expenses and savings goals.

Instructions:

1. Use the 50-30-20 budgeting rule to allocate your income to cover needs, wants, and savings.
2. Fill in the blanks with your budgeted amounts for each category.
3. Calculate the total of your budgeted expenses and compare it to your monthly income to ensure you are following the 50-30-20 guideline.
4. After completing your budget, reflect on your choices and adjust if necessary.

Income: Monthly Income: $3,000

Needs (50% of Income):

1. Rent/Mortgage: _____
2. Utilities (electricity, water, etc.): _____
3. Transportation (car payment, gas, etc.): _____
4. Groceries/Food: _____
5. Insurance (health, car, etc.): _____

Wants (30% of Income):

1. Dining Out/Entertainment: _____
2. Shopping/Clothing: _____
3. Travel/Vacation: _____
4. Personal Care/Beauty: _____
5. Hobbies/Leisure: _____

Savings (20% of Income):

1. Emergency Fund: _____
2. Retirement Savings/401(k): _____
3. Debt Repayment (if applicable): _____
4. Other Savings Goals (e.g., down payment for a house, investments): _____

Reflection:

1. How did using the 50-30-20 budgeting rule influence your budgeting decisions compared to a traditional budget?

2. Did you find it challenging to allocate your income according to the 50-30-20 guideline? Explain.

3. Are there any categories where you had to adjust to the rule? How did you prioritize your expenses?

4. What strategies will you use to ensure you stick to your budget and achieve your financial goals?

Instructions for Reflection: Reflect on your experience using the 50-30-20 budgeting rule and answer the reflection questions provided. Consider how this budgeting method can help you manage your finances effectively and plan.

Handout J:
Zero-Based Budgeting Exercise Worksheet

Scenario: You are a young professional starting your career with a monthly income of $2,500 after taxes. You have decided to use zero-based budgeting to manage your finances and ensure every dollar has a purpose.

Instructions:

1. Use zero-based budgeting to allocate your income to cover expenses, savings, and investments.
2. Assign every dollar of your income to a specific category, ensuring that your budget balances to zero.
3. Fill in the blanks with your budgeted amounts for each category.
4. After completing your budget, reflect on your choices and adjust if necessary.

Income: Monthly Income: $2,500

Expenses:

1. Rent/Mortgage: _____
2. Utilities (electricity, water, etc.): _____
3. Transportation (car payment, gas, etc.): _____
4. Groceries/Food: _____
5. Dining Out/Entertainment: _____
6. Health Insurance: _____
7. Retirement Savings/401(k): _____
8. Emergency Fund: _____
9. Debt Repayment (if applicable): _____
10. Personal Care/Beauty: _____
11. Clothing/Shopping: _____
12. Travel/Vacation: _____
13. Miscellaneous Expenses: _____

Reflection:

1. What was your experience with zero-based budgeting? Did you find it challenging to assign every dollar to a specific category?
2. Did you prioritize certain categories over others when allocating your income? Why or why not?

3. Are there any categories where you had to make trade-offs or sacrifices to ensure your budget balanced to zero?

4. How do you plan to monitor your expenses and track your progress towards your financial goals using zero-based budgeting?

Instructions for Reflection: Reflect on your budgeting experience using zero-based budgeting and answer the reflection questions provided. Consider how this budgeting method can help you take control of your finances and achieve your long-term goals.

Day 6 Lesson Plan: Saving and Investing

Grade Level: High School

Duration: 60 minutes

Objective: Students will differentiate between saving and investing, identify various investment options, and evaluate the benefits and risks associated with each.

Materials:

- Presentation slides or whiteboard and markers
- Handouts on different investment options
- Investment simulation game materials (optional)

Warm-Up (5 minutes):

- Begin the lesson by asking students to define saving and investing. Discuss their responses as a class.
- Explain the importance of both saving and investing in achieving financial goals.

Introduction to Investing (10 minutes):

1. Present a brief overview of the difference between saving and investing:
   - Saving: Putting money aside in safe, accessible accounts like savings accounts or certificates of deposit (CDs).
   - Investing: Putting money into assets such as stocks, bonds, mutual funds, or real estate with the expectation of earning a return.

2. Discuss the reasons why people invest, such as:
   - Building wealth
   - Funding retirement
   - Achieving financial goals (e.g., buying a house, paying for education)

Types of Investments (20 minutes):

1. Introduce various investment options and their characteristics:
   - Stocks: Ownership shares in a company, offering potential for high returns but also higher risk.
   - Bonds: Loans made to governments or corporations, offering fixed interest payments and lower risk compared to stocks.
   - Mutual funds: Pooled investments managed by professionals, offering diversification across multiple assets.

- Real estate: Investment in property or land, offering potential for appreciation and rental income.
2. Provide examples and explain the advantages and disadvantages of each investment type.
3. Distribute handouts or show slides with additional information on each investment option for reference.

Activity: Investment Simulation Game (20 minutes):

- Divide students into small groups.
- Provide each group with a fictional scenario (e.g., they have $10,000 to invest) and different investment options.
- Instruct students to discuss and decide how they would allocate their funds among the investment options, considering factors such as risk tolerance, investment goals, and time horizon.
- Encourage students to justify their decisions based on the information provided.

Wrap-Up and Discussion (5 minutes):

- Reconvene as a class and have each group share their investment strategies and rationale.
- Facilitate a discussion on the importance of diversification, risk management, and long-term planning in investing.
- Summarize key takeaways from the lesson and address any remaining questions.

Homework (if applicable):

- Assign a reflection or research task where students explore one investment option in more depth and report back to the class in the next lesson.

Additional Elements:

- Consider inviting a guest speaker, such as a financial advisor or investment professional, to provide insights and answer student questions.
- Incorporate real-world examples and case studies of successful investors or investment strategies to enhance engagement and relevance.
- Utilize online investment simulation platforms or stock market games to provide hands-on experience with investing in a simulated environment.

Handout K
Investment Simulation Game Handout

Scenario: You and your group have been given $10,000 to invest. Your task is to decide how to allocate this money among various investment options. Consider factors such as risk, return, and your investment goals when making your decisions.

Investment Options:

1. **Stocks (Company A):**
    - Description: Ownership shares in a well-established tech company with a history of robust performance.
    - Potential Return: High returns, but also higher risk due to market volatility.
    - Investment Amount: $_____ (Enter amount allocated)

2. **Bonds (Government Bonds):**
    - Description: Loans made to the government with a fixed interest rate and guaranteed principal repayment.
    - Potential Return: Moderate returns, lower risk compared to stocks.
    - Investment Amount: $_____ (Enter amount allocated)

3. **Mutual Funds (Diversified Portfolio):**
    - Description: Professionally managed investment fund that pools money from multiple investors to invest in a diversified portfolio of stocks and bonds.
    - Potential Return: Moderate to high returns, depending on the fund's performance.
    - Investment Amount: $_____ (Enter amount allocated)

4. **Real Estate (Rental Property):**
    - Description: Investment in a rental property in a growing urban area.
    - Potential Return: Rental income and potential property appreciation over time.
    - Investment Amount: $_____ (Enter amount allocated)

5. **Stocks (Company B):**
    1. Description: Ownership shares in a pharmaceutical company specializing in innovative drug development.
    2. Potential Return: Moderate to high returns, with some volatility based on industry performance and regulatory factors.
    3. Investment Amount: $_____ (Enter amount allocated)

6. **Bonds (Corporate Bonds):**
    1. Description: Loans made to a well-established multinational corporation, offering a fixed interest rate and periodic coupon payments.
    2. Potential Return: Moderate returns, slightly higher risk compared to government bonds due to issuer credit risk.
    3. Investment Amount: $_____ (Enter amount allocated)

Investment Strategy: Discuss with your group and decide how you will allocate the $10,000 among the investment options listed above. Consider the following questions:

- What are your investment goals? (e.g., short-term vs. long-term, income generation, capital appreciation)
- What is your risk tolerance? How comfortable are you with potential fluctuations in the value of your investments?
- How will you diversify your portfolio to manage risk?
- What factors will you consider when evaluating the potential return of each investment option?
- How will you balance the trade-off between risk and return?

Instructions:

1. Allocate the $10,000 among the investment options by entering the amount you wish to invest in each category.
2. Justify your investment decisions based on the information provided and your group's discussion.
3. Be prepared to present your investment strategy to the class and explain your rationale.

Investment Allocation:

1. Stocks (Company A): $_____
2. Bonds (Government Bonds): $_____
3. Mutual Funds (Diversified Portfolio): $_____
4. Real Estate (Rental Property): $_____
5. Stocks (Company B): $_____
6. Bonds (Corporate Bonds): _____

Rationale for Investment Decisions:

1. Stocks (Company A): _____
2. Bonds (Government Bonds): _____
3. Mutual Funds (Diversified Portfolio): _____
4. Real Estate (Rental Property): _____
5. Stocks (Company B): $_____
6. Bonds (Corporate Bonds):_____

Note: Total investment amounts should add up to $10,000.

_____

(Group Leader Signature)

_____

(Group Member Signature)

_____

(Group Member Signature)

_____

(Group Member Signature)

Handout L

First Round Investment Results:

1. **Stocks (Company A):**

    - Description: Company A, a leading tech firm, experienced a 10% gain in the first round due to strong quarterly earnings and positive market sentiment in the tech sector.

2. **Bonds (Government Bonds):**

    - Description: Government bonds saw a modest 2% return in the first round, providing stability to investors amid market volatility.

3. **Mutual Funds (Diversified Portfolio):**

    - Description: The diversified portfolio of mutual funds delivered a solid 8% return in the first round, benefiting from a balanced allocation across various asset classes.

4. **Real Estate (Rental Property):**

    - Description: Rental property investments remained steady with a 3% return in the first round, driven by consistent rental income and moderate property appreciation.

5. **Stocks (Company B):**

    - Description: Company B, a pharmaceutical innovator, faced a slight setback with a 5% loss in the first round due to regulatory challenges affecting its product pipeline.

6. **Bonds (Corporate Bonds):**

    - Description: Corporate bonds experienced a 4% gain in the first round, reflecting the strong financial performance of the issuing corporations and investor demand for higher yields.

Considerations for Round 2:

- **Company Performance:** Evaluate the recent performance and outlook for each investment option, considering factors such as earnings reports, market trends, and industry developments.

- **Risk Assessment:** Assess the level of risk associated with each investment option and determine whether adjustments are needed to align with your risk tolerance and investment objectives.

- **Diversification:** Review the diversification of your portfolio and consider rebalancing to ensure a well-rounded mix of assets that can weather market fluctuations.

- **Market Conditions:** Stay informed about current market conditions and economic indicators that may impact investment returns, including interest rates, inflation, and geopolitical events.

- **Long-Term Goals:** Revisit your long-term investment goals and adjust your strategy, accordingly, balancing the need for growth with the preservation of capital over time.

- **Opportunistic Investments:** Look for opportunities to capitalize on market inefficiencies or undervalued assets that may offer attractive returns in the current environment.

Instructions for Round 2:

1. Reallocate the $10,000 among the investment options for Round 2 based on your updated assessment and considerations.

2. Justify your investment decisions for Round 2 and explain how they reflect changes in market conditions and your investment objectives.

3. Be prepared to present your updated investment strategy to the class, highlighting the rationale behind your decisions and any adjustments made from Round 1.

Investment Allocation for Round 2:

1. Stocks (Company A): $_____
2. Bonds (Government Bonds): $_____
3. Mutual Funds (Diversified Portfolio): $_____
4. Real Estate (Rental Property): $_____
5. Stocks (Company B): $_____
6. Bonds (Corporate Bonds): $_____

Rationale for Round 2 Investment Decisions:

1. Stocks (Company A): _____
2. Bonds (Government Bonds): _____
3. Mutual Funds (Diversified Portfolio): _____
4. Real Estate (Rental Property): _____
5. Stocks (Company B): _____
6. Bonds (Corporate Bonds): _____

Note: Total investment amounts should add up to $10,000 for Round 2.

(Group Leader Signature)

(Group Member Signature)

(Group Member Signature)

(Group Member Signature)

Round 2 Investment Results:

1. **Stocks (Company A):**
    - Description: Despite initial optimism, Company A faced challenges in the second round, resulting in a 5% loss. This downturn was influenced by a slowdown in the tech sector and concerns over supply chain disruptions.

2. **Bonds (Government Bonds):**
    - Description: Government bonds continued to provide stability in the second round, delivering a steady 2% return. Investors sought the safety of bonds amidst ongoing market volatility and economic uncertainty.

3. **Mutual Funds (Diversified Portfolio):**
    - Description: The diversified portfolio of mutual funds outperformed expectations with a strong 10% gain in the second round. This was driven by robust performances across various sectors, including technology, healthcare, and renewable energy.

4. **Real Estate (Rental Property):**
    - Description: Rental property investments maintained their steady performance, generating a 3% return in the second round. This resilience was attributed to consistent rental income and favorable market conditions in the housing sector.

5. **Stocks (Company B):**
    - Description: Company B experienced a turnaround in the second round, rebounding with a 7% gain. Positive developments in its product pipeline and successful regulatory approvals boosted investor confidence and drove stock prices higher.

6. **Bonds (Corporate Bonds):**
    - Description: Corporate bonds delivered a moderate 4% return in the second round, reflecting stable corporate earnings and investor demand for fixed-income securities amidst uncertain market conditions.

Overall Portfolio Performance:

- Total Portfolio Return: *(Calculate the overall return percentage for the entire portfolio based on the performance of each investment option in Round 2.)*

Reflection and Analysis:

- Discuss how the results of Round 2 compared to your expectations and initial investment strategy.
- Analyze the factors that influenced the performance of each investment option, including market trends, economic indicators, and company-specific developments.

- Reflect on the effectiveness of your diversification strategy and its impact on managing risk and maximizing returns.
- Consider any adjustments or lessons learned from Round 2 that may inform future investment decisions.

Handout M

Investment Simulation Game Closure Worksheet

Name:_____

Date:_____

Instructions: Reflect on your experience participating in the investment simulation game. Answer the following questions to summarize your learning and insights gained from the activity.

1. What were your initial investment goals when participating in the simulation game? Did your goals change throughout the activity? Explain any shifts in your investment objectives.

2. Describe one investment option that performed better than expected in the simulation game. What factors do you think contributed to its success?

3. Identify one investment option that underperformed in the simulation game. What challenges or obstacles did this investment face, and what lessons did you learn from its performance?

4. Reflect on the importance of diversification in managing investment risk. How did diversifying your portfolio impact your overall investment strategy and performance in the simulation game?

5. Discuss any surprises or unexpected outcomes you encountered during the simulation game. How did these experiences shape your understanding of investing and financial decision-making?

6. Based on your participation in the simulation game, what are some key takeaways or lessons learned about investing and personal finance that you can apply to real-life situations?

7. What are some steps you can take to continue learning about investing and improving your financial literacy beyond the simulation game?

8. Overall, how did you find the investment simulation game experience? What aspects did you enjoy the most, and what areas do you think could be improved for future iterations of the activity?

9. Optional: Is there any additional feedback or comments you would like to share about the investment simulation game activity?

Day 7 Lesson Plan: Incorporating "The Price is Right" Games

Duration: 60 minutes

Objective:

- Students will analyze "The Price is Right" games to identify economic principles and personal finance concepts.
- Students will discuss the relevance of these games in understanding real-world economic decision-making.

Materials:

- Video clips from "The Price is Right" (selected in advance)
- Whiteboard and markers
- Handout with guiding questions
- Projector or screen for video clips

Introduction (5 minutes):

1. Greet the students and introduce the topic of the day: "Incorporating 'The Price is Right' Games into Economics and Personal Finance."
2. Explain that today's lesson will focus on analyzing popular games from "The Price is Right" and discussing how they relate to economic principles and personal finance concepts.

Activity 1: Analyzing "The Price is Right" Games (25 minutes):

1. Divide the class into small groups (3-4 students per group).
2. Distribute the handout with guiding questions to each group.
3. Show video clips of selected "The Price is Right" games that highlight economic decision-making or personal finance scenarios.
4. In their groups, students watch the clips and discuss the following questions:
    - What economic principles are at play in this game?
    - How do the contestants' decisions relate to personal finance concepts?
    - What can we learn from this game about consumer behavior, pricing strategies, or financial decision-making?
5. Encourage students to take notes and prepare to share their observations with the class.

Activity 2: Group Discussion (20 minutes):

1. Bring the class back together for a whole-group discussion.
2. Ask each group to share their observations and insights from the video clips.

3. Facilitate a discussion around the following points:
   - Common economic principles illustrated in "The Price is Right" games.
   - How contestants' behavior reflects personal finance concepts such as budgeting, risk-taking, and opportunity cost.
   - The role of pricing strategies and incentives in consumer decision-making.
   - Any ethical considerations raised by the games.
4. Summarize the key takeaways from the discussion and emphasize the relevance of understanding these concepts in everyday life.

Conclusion (5 minutes):

1. Review the main points covered in the lesson.
2. Reinforce the importance of applying economic and personal finance principles to make informed decisions.
3. Assign any follow-up activities or readings related to the lesson topic.

Assessment:

- Participation in group discussions and sharing of insights.
- Completion of the handout with thoughtful responses.
- Engagement in whole-class discussion and contributions to the analysis of "The Price is Right" games.

Extension:

- As an extension activity, students could research and analyze additional episodes of "The Price is Right" on their own, focusing on different games and their economic implications.
- Students could also create their own game show-style activities or simulations that illustrate economic principles and personal finance concepts for their classmates to participate in.

Handout N

The Price is Right: Game On!

Welcome, contestants! Today's episode is all about understanding economics and personal finance through the lens of classic Price is Right games.

Round 1: Plinko Plunge!

Watch the clip: A contestant excitedly drops chips down the iconic Plinko board, hoping to land prizes with varying values.

Think Like an Economist:

- **Supply & Demand:** How does the limited number of spaces on the board impact the value of prizes?
- **Marginal Cost & Benefit:** With each chip, is the potential reward worth the risk of landing on a small prize?
- **Scarcity:** Does the excitement around "big-ticket" prizes influence contestant behavior?

Finance in Action:

- **Budgeting:** Does this game require strategic budgeting of chip drops for maximum benefit?
- **Risk Tolerance:** Are contestants playing it safe or taking calculated risks with their chip placement?
- **Opportunity Cost:** What is the "cost" of aiming for a high-value prize versus aiming for multiple smaller prizes?

Discuss with your team:

- Did the contestant prioritize high-risk, high-reward plays or safe, consistent choices?
- How could this be connected to budgeting for long-term financial goals?

Round 2: Cliff Hangers!

Watch the clip: Contestants bid on a brand-new car, inching closer to the actual price without going over.

Think Like an Economist:

- **Market Equilibrium:** How does the bidding process determine the purchase price of the car?
- **Incentives:** What motivates contestants to bid strategically, even when losing?
- **Information Asymmetry:** Do contestants have all the information needed to make the most informed bid?

Finance in Action:

- **Negotiation:** Are there any negotiation strategies used by the contestants?

- **Impulse Buying:** Does the excitement of the game influence emotional spending decisions?
- **Opportunity Cost:** What could they have spent the bid money on if they didn't win the car?

Discuss with your team:

- What factors did contestants consider beyond the car's actual value?
- How does this relate to responsible budgeting and avoiding impulse purchases?

Bonus Round: Think Tank Time!

Create your own Price is Right game! Design a game that showcases an economic principle or personal finance concept. Share your game with the class and explain how it connects to real-world financial decisions.

Remember: Be creative, have fun, and keep in mind the economic and financial concepts we've discussed!

Day 8 Lesson Plan: Plinko Budgeting Challenge

Objectives:

- Students will understand the importance of allocating income across different spending categories.
- Students will recognize the role of chance and uncertainty in budgeting and financial planning.
- Students will practice decision-making skills on where to allocate resources within a budget.

Materials:

- A large Plinko board (constructed or borrowed)
- Tokens or discs to represent funds
- Whiteboard and markers
- "Plinko Budgeting Worksheet" for each student (designed by you, see example below)

Procedure:

1. **Warm-up and Review (10 minutes):**
    - Briefly review the key principles of budgeting from previous lessons.
    - Ask students: "When creating a budget, what are some important spending categories to consider?"
    - Introduce the concept of uncertainty or unexpected events affecting a budget.

2. **Introducing Plinko Budgeting (15 minutes):**
    - Explain the traditional rules of Plinko.
    - Adapt the game for budgeting:
        - Each slot at the bottom of the board will represent a spending category (e.g., housing, food, transportation, entertainment, savings, etc.).
        - Assign different "values" to each slot based on typical budget priorities (e.g., higher values for necessities like housing, lower for entertainment).
    - Discuss how randomness in Plinko simulates real-life budget variations.

3. **Plinko Budgeting Game (20 minutes):**
    - Distribute "Plinko Budgeting Worksheets" (see example below).
    - Give each student a set number of tokens/discs to represent a fictional income amount.
    - In turns, students drop discs on the Plinko board one by one.
    - On their worksheets, they record where each disc lands and the corresponding budget category and value.

4. **Analysis & Discussion (15 minutes)**
    - Once all students have played, calculate their "budgets" based on the Plinko results.
    - Questions for discussion:
        - Did your budget end up balanced? Did you face any surpluses or shortages in categories?
        - How realistic was this simulation? Were you happy with how your funds were allocated?
        - How does randomness or chance affect real-life budgets?
        - What strategies could you use to mitigate unexpected occurrences in budgeting?
5. **Wrap-up (5 minutes):**
    - Emphasize that while budgets can be affected by unforeseen events, careful planning and prioritization are essential for responsible financial management.

Differentiation

- **Advanced:** Have students write short justifications on why they'd want to increase or decrease funds in particular categories given their results
- **Support:** Provide pre-filled budget categories and priority rankings, so students focus on the distribution.

Assessment:

- Participation in game and discussion
- Plinko Budgeting Worksheets
- Exit ticket: Ask students to name one thing they learned about budgeting through the Plinko game.

Handout O

Plinko Budgeting Worksheet

Name:

Date:

Instructions

1. **Starting Income:** Everyone begins with 3 tokens.
2. **Optional Bonus Activities:** Complete up to TWO activities below to earn additional tokens (1 token per activity).
3. **Plinko Time:** Drop your tokens on the Plinko board, one at a time.
4. **Record & Analyze:** On the chart, note where each token lands and calculate your budget. Then answer the analysis questions.

Budgeting Chart

Disc #	Category Landed In	Value of Slot
1 (Starting)	Needs	
2 (Starting)	Wants	
3 (Starting)	Saving	
4 (Optional)		
5 (Optional)		

Total Income:

Optional Bonus Activities (Choose one or both)

- **Activity 1: Market Mayhem**
    - Scenario: You work part-time at a store. Due to economic factors, many shoppers reduce their spending, leading to fewer hours offered for part-time staff. How might this impact your personal budget, and what are some short-term actions you could take to adjust?

- **Activity 2: Investment Speculation**
    - You hear about a new company going public (offering stock). Research a current trend (e.g., rise of plant-based foods, advancements in AI). Name a hypothetical company that fits this trend. Why might investing in them be risky, but potentially rewarding?

Budget Analysis Questions

1. Is your budget balanced? Are there any surpluses or shortages?

2. Which categories received the most/least funding? Why?

3. Did the bonus activities significantly change your budget? Explain.

4. How can you plan for unexpected events that might disrupt your budget in real life?

Day 9 Lesson Plan: Spin the Wheel of Investments

Objectives:

- Students will understand the concept of investment returns and the varying levels of risk associated with different investment types.
- Students will analyze the trade-off between potential rewards and risks in investment decisions.
- Students will practice investment decision-making through a game-based simulation.

Materials:

- Large "Spin the Wheel" (can be constructed, repurposed, or use an online virtual wheel)
- Whiteboard and markers
- "Investment Portfolio Tracker" worksheet for each student (designed by you, see example below)
- Diverse assortment of "investment" examples (stocks, real estate, etc.) with their potential returns and associated risks clearly noted

Procedure

1. **Warm-up and Intro (10 minutes):**
   - Review key terms: investment, risk, return, diversification.
   - Pose the question: "If you had $1,000 to invest, would you put it all into one potentially high-growth stock, or spread it across safer investments with lower returns?"
   - Introduce the "Spin the Wheel of Investments" activity.

2. **Setting Up the Wheel (10 minutes)**
   - Divide the wheel into segments representing different investment options you've pre-selected (e.g., stable bonds, tech stocks, a savings account, real estate venture, etc.).
   - Assign realistic return percentages to each segment. Include some high-return (high-risk) and some low-return (low-risk) options.
   - Briefly explain each investment type & its risk potential.

3. **Spin & invest! (20 minutes)**
   - Distribute the "Investment Portfolio Tracker" worksheets.
   - Students begin with a set amount of fictional money to invest.
   - In turns, students "spin" the wheel. The sector their spin lands on is the investment they must "purchase."
   - Students record their investment options and the corresponding (positive or negative) returns on their tracker sheets.

4. **Portfolio Analysis (15 minutes)**
    - After multiple rounds, have students calculate their total portfolio value (initial investment + gains/losses).
    - Discussion Questions:
        - Who experienced the highest returns? Who took the biggest risks to achieve this?
        - Does a higher return always mean a better investment? Why or why not?
        - How does diversification (having a mix of investments) play a role?
        - Did anyone's strategy change as they played?

5. **Wrap-Up (5 minutes)**
    - Emphasize: There's no single "winning" investment strategy – it depends on individual risk tolerance and goals.

Differentiation:

- **Scaffold:** Add a column for writing justifications on why someone might choose (or avoid) investments.
- **Challenge:** Have students research historical return rates to increase the realism of their simulation.

Assessment:

- Participation in the game and discussion
- Completed Investment Portfolio Tracker worksheets
- Short reflection: Would a student use a similar strategy if investing real money? Why or why not?

Wheel Setup

Materials:

- **Your Wheel:** This can be constructed from cardboard, an old game spinner, or use an online "wheel of fortune" (I recommend wheelofnames.com) type website where you can input the segments.

- **Investment Explanation Handout:** A handout explaining the general idea of each segment for student reference.

Wheel Setup:

1. **Divide:** Divide your wheel into 25 roughly equal segments.

2. **Labeling:** Here's a suggested segment distribution:

    - **High-Return, High-Risk Stock (5 segments):** Label these prominently or with a visually "exciting" color (e.g., bright yellow).

    - **Medium-Return, Medium-Risk Stock (5 segments):** Less flashy than high-risk, but clearly distinct (e.g., light blue).

    - **Low-Return, Low-Risk Stock/ Bond (5 segments)** Visually "stable" (e.g., pale green).

    - **Savings Account (4 segments):** Color indicating safety (e.g., grey).

    - **"Surprise" (3 segments):** Fun color choice (e.g., bright pink)

    - **"Bust" (3 segments):** Visually negative (e.g., bold red).

3. **Assign Returns:** Now, for each segment type, you'll need returns:

    - High-Risk: +20%, +15%, +10% variations, also some -10%, -15%

    - Medium Risk: +8%, +5%, variations, smaller negatives of -3%, -5%

    - Low Risk: Mostly +2%, +3%, maybe an occasional -1%

    - Savings: Flat +1%

    - Surprise: This depends on how generous you want it to be!

    - Bust: Segments here could be -50% or even -100% (lose the whole investment)

Handout P
Understanding Your Investment Options

Stocks: Owning a Piece of the Action

- Imagine a company is like a pie. Stocks are slices of that pie – you own a tiny piece of the business!
- If the company does well, your slice could become more valuable (high-risk, high-reward).
- But if the company struggles, your slice might shrink (potential to lose money).

Bonds: Lending a Helping Hand

- Think of bonds like an IOU. You lend money to a company or government, and they promise to pay you back with interest (a little extra on top).
- Bonds are generally safer than stocks – you're likely to get your money back.
- But the extra interest they pay is generally small (lower returns).

Savings Accounts: Safe and Steady

- The safest place to stash your cash. Your money is protected, and it earns a tiny bit of interest.
- Great for emergency funds or short-term savings goals.
- But won't grow your money as fast as other investments might.

Surprise: The Wild Card

- This segment on the wheel is a mystery!
- It could represent investing in a hot new trend, or something very unpredictable.
- Highest risk, but also the possibility of the highest reward.

Bust: When Things Go Wrong

- Uh-oh! Sometimes even big companies struggle, or unexpected events shake up the market.
- A "bust" means a bad turn of events that causes your investment to lose value.
- This highlights the reality that all investments carry some level of risk.

Key Points to Remember

- **Risk vs. Reward:** Generally, the higher the potential reward (making lots of money), the higher the risk (potential to lose money).
- **Your Goals Matter:** How quickly do you need the money? Are you okay with ups and downs or do you need something super stable?

This is just a quick intro – there's an entire world of investments to explore!

Handout Q

Investment Portfolio Tracker

Name:

Date:

Starting Investment Amount: $ 1000

Instructions

1. **Plan Your Portfolio:** Before any spins, allocate your money across different investment types.
2. **Spin & Adjust:** After each round, track any gains/losses and update your portfolio value.
3. **Reflect:** Answer the questions below after the game ends.

Initial Portfolio Allocation

Investment Type	Amount Invested	Why you chose this amount
High-Risk Stock		
Medium-Risk Stock		
Low-Risk Stock/Bond		
Savings Account		
TOTAL (Must equal your starting amount)		

Investment Tracker

Round # 1	Spin Result	Gain/Loss Amount	Current Portfolio Value
1			
2			
3			
4			
5			
Total Gain/Loss			

Start of Round 2 Portfolio Allocation

Investment Type	Amount Invested	Why you chose this amount
High-Risk Stock		
Medium-Risk Stock		
Low-Risk Stock/Bond		
Savings Account		
TOTAL		

Investment Tracker

Round # 2	Spin Result	Gain/Loss Amount	Current Portfolio Value
1			
2			
3			
4			
5			

Reflection Questions

1. Did your initial investment strategy work out as you expected? Why or why not?

2. Which investment type proved the most/least successful for you?

3. Were you surprised by any outcomes? Did this change how you invest in the future?

4. Does this game make you interested in real-life investing? Explain.

Day 10 Lesson Plan: Tackling Real-World Financial Decisions
Objectives:

- Students will apply the economic and personal finance concepts learned throughout the unit to critically analyze real-world scenarios.

- Students will develop recommendations and solutions for financial challenges.
- Students will practice presentation and communication skills in sharing their analyses.

Materials:

- Scenario handouts (see preparation notes below)
- Whiteboard or projector for displaying scenarios (optional)
- Presentation rubric or guidelines for students
- Any resources students might need for presentations (visual aids, technology)

Procedure

1. **Warm-Up: Brainstorm & Connect (10 minutes)**
   - As a class, brainstorm a list of real-world financial decisions individuals and businesses face (buying a house, budgeting amidst rising costs, starting a business, etc.)
   - Ask: What economic and personal finance concepts we've studied would be relevant for analyzing these decisions?

2. **Group Presentation Introductions (10 minutes)**
   - Explain that each group will be showcasing their analysis of a specific real-world scenario related to the unit's themes.
   - Briefly summarize the presentation expectations or review your rubric
   - Allow time for a brief Q&A to clarify expectations.

3. **Presentations & Peer Feedback (50-60 minutes – adjust based on group number)**
   - Each group presents their scenario analysis (time limits depend on your class size)
   - Facilitate constructive feedback after each presentation:
     - Two things they found insightful about the analysis
     - One question they have or a suggestion for improvement.

4. **Wrap-Up Discussion (10 minutes)**
   - Which scenario resonated with students the most? Why?
   - Did any presentations bring up unexpected ideas or perspectives?
   - How does this activity reinforce the importance of the unit's concepts for real-world decision-making?

Preparation: Scenario Development

- **Scenario Sources:** Find scenarios relating to your unit's focus:

- News articles (rising inflation, housing market shifts)
- Fictional case studies you create (teen managing income, a business considering expansion)
- Online resources designed for teaching economics/finance

- **Varying Complexity:** Include scenarios with different difficulty levels to suit your groups.
- **Required Analysis:** For each scenario, outline questions or analysis goals students must address within their presentations.

Presentation Tips:

- **Time Limits:** Be firm! This keeps things moving.
- **Visual Aids:** Are visual aids (graphs, brief PowerPoint, etc.) encouraged or even required?
- **Audience Role:** Are audience members jotting notes for feedback, or simply engaged listening?

Assessment:

- Group Presentations (using your rubric, focusing on concept application, recommendations, communication)
- Individual Reflection: After all presentations, students reflect on what they learned from both their own analysis and their peers' work.

Presentation Rubric

Criteria	4 - Exemplary	3 - Proficient	2 - Developing	1 - Needs Improvement
Concept Application	Uses multiple economic and personal finance concepts with a clear understanding of their connection to the real-world scenario.	Accurately uses relevant concepts, showing a solid understanding of their relationship to the scenario.	Shows some understanding of relevant concepts, but connections to the scenario might be unclear or simplistic.	Struggles to identify appropriate concepts or demonstrates major misunderstandings.
Analysis & Recommendations	Presents a thorough analysis of the scenario, considering multiple perspectives, and offers well-justified recommendations.	Provides a thoughtful analysis of the scenario and offers sound recommendations.	Analysis is present but may lack depth or overlook some important considerations.	Analysis is incomplete or overly simplistic. Recommendations are poorly supported.
Organization & Clarity	The presentation is clear, well-structured, and flows logically. Ideas are presented with excellent clarity.	The presentation has a clear structure, and the main points are easy to follow.	The presentation's organization could be stronger, making it harder to follow at times. Clarity could be improved.	The presentation lacks organization and is difficult to follow. Major clarity issues.
Delivery & Engagement	Group members all speak confidently, maintain eye contact, and their delivery actively engages the audience.	Group members present with good speaking skills and generally connect with the audience.	Some members present confidently, but overall delivery could be stronger. Audience engagement is lacking.	Delivery is poor (mumbling, reading directly from notes) and disconnects the audience

Example Scenarios

Scenario 1: The Housing Decision

- **Focus:** Opportunity cost, market analysis, personal budgeting
- **Article:** Young Families Are Fleeing the Housing Market: https://www.washingtonpost.com/business/interactive/2023/housing-market-price-trends/
- **Scenario:** You are a recent college graduate considering two job offers. One is in a major city with a higher salary but extremely high rent. The other is in a smaller town with a lower salary but affordable housing options.
- **Task:** Analyze the financial trade-offs of each option, considering factors beyond salary. Research typical rental costs in each location. Create a budget for each scenario. Recommend an option, justifying your decision with economic reasoning.

Scenario 2: Business Expansion

- **Focus:** Supply and demand, market opportunities, investment
- **Article:** Supply Chain Issues Persist: https://www.bbc.co.uk/news/topics/c96g579rr6xt
- **Scenario:** You run a small online crafts business experiencing increased demand. Unfortunately, there's a shortage of your core supplies, driving up costs.
- **Task:** Research alternative suppliers or substitute materials. Weigh the pros and cons of raising prices to cover costs vs. maintaining pricing and risking reduced profit margins. Evaluate whether investing in expanding production capacity makes sense given potential future supply problems.

Scenario 3: The Impact of Inflation

- **Focus:** Macroeconomics, inflation's effects, budgeting adjustments
- **Article:** How rising inflation is complicating budgeting, retirement planning: [[invalid URL removed]]([invalid URL removed])
- **Scenario:** You're responsible for your family's grocery budget. With rising inflation, the cost of food has increased significantly.
- **Task:** Research which food categories have seen the largest price hikes. Propose strategies to keep grocery costs down (adjusting buying habits, seeking alternatives, etc.). Discuss the broader economic factors driving inflation.

Scenario 4: Student Loan Strategy

- **Focus:** Personal finance, debt management, interest rates
- **Article:** Biden cancels up to $20,000 in student loan debt: https://www.npr.org/2023/08/08/1192703211/biden-save-plan-how-it-works

- **Scenario:** You're graduating with $25,000 in student loans. You're offered a few repayment options (standard 10-year plan, income-based repayment, etc.). News articles suggest possible student loan forgiveness plans.
- **Task:** Research repayment options, compare total interest paid overtime. Discuss the benefits of paying aggressively vs. waiting for potential forgiveness (consider current political climate).

Scenario 5: Investing Debate

- **Focus:** Investing basics, risk tolerance, economic indicators
- **Article:** Experts differ on whether it's a suitable time to invest amid ongoing market swings: https://www.npr.org/2022/09/28/1125656030/the-markets-are-down-heres-how-to-handle-your-investments
- **Scenario:** You've inherited $10,000. Advisors are split on whether it's a suitable time to invest in the stock market due to volatility.
- **Task:** Define your risk tolerance. Research economic indicators to argue for OR against investing immediately. Recommend a potential investment strategy (or non-investment option) and justify your reasoning.

Scenario 6: Ethical Business Choice

- **Focus:** Opportunity cost, corporate responsibility, microeconomics
- **Article:** Companies struggle to balance 'doing good' with making money: https://www.forbes.com/sites/forbesfinancecouncil/2023/02/14/how-ethical-business-tactics-can-improve-profitability/
- **Scenario:** Your company could increase profits significantly by outsourcing production to a country with lower labor costs, but working conditions and wages there are concerning.
- **Task:** Analyze the economic and ethical implications. Consider short-term gains vs. potential damage to brand reputation. Argue for OR against outsourcing, considering economic principles and ethical considerations.

Handout R

Scenario Analysis Guide

Group Members:

Scenario Title/Source:

How to Use This Guide:

1. Work through these questions as a group. Not every question requires a written answer but be prepared to discuss your responses.
2. Use your textbook, notes, and online resources to aid your analysis.
3. Prepare to present your key findings and your final recommendation.

1. Identifying the Key Problem/Decision:

- Briefly summarize the central issue or decision faced in the scenario. Is this primarily an economic problem or a personal finance problem (or a combination)?

- Who is the primary decision-maker (an individual, business, etc.)?

2. Relevant Economic & Personal Finance Concepts

- List ALL economic or personal finance concepts from our unit that could apply to this situation (Examples: scarcity, budgeting, investment, supply/demand, risk/reward, inflation, opportunity cost, etc.)

    o Circle the 3-4 concepts MOST crucial for understanding and solving this scenario. Be prepared to explain why you selected these.

3. Analyzing the Situation

- **Opportunity Cost:** What are the potential trade-offs involved in the choices facing the decision-maker?

- **Economic Factors:**
  - Are there specific market forces (supply/demand for certain goods) influencing this scenario?
  - Are there broader economic trends (inflation, recession) that the decision-maker must consider?

- **Personal Finance Factors:**
  - Does the scenario involve budgeting, saving, or managing debt?
  - What are the potential financial risks involved, and how can they be mitigated?

4. Developing Recommendations

- **Goals:** What does the decision-maker hope to achieve (maximize profit, reduce expenses, minimize risk, etc.)? Be specific.

- **Feasibility:** Can your solution realistically be implemented given the time, resources, and other constraints present in the scenario?

- **Justification:** Use the economic and personal finance concepts you identified earlier to explain why your recommendation is the best course of action.

5. Additional Considerations/Unknowns

- Are there any ethical implications associated with the possible solutions?

- What important pieces of information do you wish you had to make an even stronger analysis?

Important Notes

- **Scenario Type:** Tailor your focus as needed. Some scenarios might be heavily focused on market analysis, while others are more centered around personal budgeting.
- **"Unknowns" Section:** Emphasizes that real-world decision-making often involves working with imperfect information.

Day 11 Lesson Plan: Putting It All Together: Your Financial Masterplan

Objectives:

- Students will review and solidify their understanding of key economic and personal finance concepts from the unit.
- Students will apply their knowledge by creating a detailed financial plan tailored to a realistic scenario.

Materials:

- Comprehensive Financial Plan Project Guidelines (see outline below)
- Whiteboard or projector for review activity
- Internet access or printed resources if needed for project work

Procedure

1. **Concept Brainstorm & Connections (15 minutes)**
    - Class brainstorm: "What are 5 BIG IDEAS from this unit that will stick with you for making important financial decisions?"
    - List these on the board. For each idea, have students quickly name at least two related concepts or vocabulary terms.
    - Highlight the interconnected nature of various concepts within the unit.

2. **Introducing the Financial Plan Project (15 minutes):**
    - Distribute the detailed project guidelines.
    - Present at least two potential scenarios students can select from (see guidelines below).
    - Explain assessment criteria: What elements are essential for a successful financial plan?
    - Allow time for clarifying questions.

3. **Project Work Time (50 - 60 minutes – flexible depending on your project scope)**
    - Students begin work on their comprehensive financial plans, individually or in groups as you've designated.
    - Circulate: offer guidance, ensure students apply concepts correctly, and answer questions.

4. **Wrap-Up (5 minutes)**
    - Clarify any ongoing project expectations or deadlines.
    - Ask a few students to share initial impressions of the project: Is it challenging? Which components are they looking forward to tackling?

Comprehensive Financial Plan Project Guidelines

- **Scenario Choices:** Provide students with two or more scenarios. Examples:
    - **Starting Out:** College graduate with their first full-time job, student loans, and goals to buy a car and start saving.
    - **Family Finances:** A new parent returning to the workforce while their partner has a fluctuating income. Need to plan for childcare, housing, etc.
- **Required Plan Elements**
    - Income Analysis (all sources)
    - Detailed Budget (using categories relevant to the scenario)
    - Saving & Debt Management Strategies
    - Short-Term & Long-Term Financial Goals (with plans to meet them)
    - Investment Component (if appropriate for the scenario)
- **Deliverable Format:** Flexibility is good! Some might use spreadsheets, some prefer outlining, visual learners might enjoy creative representations of their plan.
- **Beyond the Numbers:** Require a section where students reflect on the connection between their financial plan and the economic concepts studied.

Assessment

- Financial plans themselves: Use a rubric to assess concept application, plan comprehensiveness, realism, and justification of decisions.
- Presentations: Allow students to briefly present their plans and explain their reasoning. (Depending on class size, this may be selective).

Sample Rubric

CATEGORY	EXEMPLARY - 4 POINTS	PROFICIENT - 3 POINTS	DEVELOPING - 2 POINTS	NEEDS IMPROVEMENT - 1 POINT
INCOME ANALYSIS	Income from all sources clearly identified and documented. Net income calculated accurately.	Income identified with accurate calculations.	Some income sources may be missing, or calculations contain minor errors.	Multiple income sources overlooked; calculations have significant errors.
BUDGETING	Budget is detailed, includes all relevant categories, and reflects realistic research on costs. Provides ample justification for spending choices.	Budget is organized and covers most spending categories, with generally realistic amounts. Justification present but could be stronger.	Budget includes major categories but lacks some specificity or overlooks certain expenses. Minimal justification.	Budget is disorganized, expenses are unrealistic, and/or missing major categories. No justification.
SAVINGS & DEBT MANAGEMENT	Clear plans for both debt repayment (if applicable) AND multiple savings goals (short-term & long term). Strategy balances these goals realistically.	Outlines a plan for savings and/or debt repayment. Goals and plan are reasonable.	Provides plan for either savings OR debt, or the plan lacks sufficient detail and clear timing.	Does not include a savings or debt repayment plan, or the plan is unrealistic given the scenario.
INVESTMENT (IF APPLICABLE)	If investment was included, it shows research into suitable options with sound justification for risk level and alignment with goals.	Investment choices align with scenario & generally sound. Justification could be clearer or more tailored.	Includes investment, but the choice seems unsuitable for the scenario or without supporting rationale.	Includes investment with no real understanding shown of how it contributes to financial goals.
CONCEPT APPLICATION	Thorough reflection demonstrates a firm grasp of economic/personal finance concepts, connecting them clearly to plan choices. Offers thoughtful insights.	Shows a good understanding of core concepts and links them to the financial plan. Reflection may lack some depth.	Demonstrates understanding of basic concepts but struggles to connect them to the plan or reflect insightfully.	Conceptual understanding appears weak, reflection is superficial or inaccurate.
ORGANIZATION & PRESENTATION	The plan is well-structured, visually clear, and easy to follow. Exceeds expectations in layout or creativity.	The plan is organized and mostly easy to follow.	Plan could be better organized, making it harder to read. Visual presentation is basic.	The plan is disorganized, and the presentation detracts from the content.

Handout S

Project: Your Financial Masterplan

The Challenge

Life is full of financial decisions, both big and small. Having a plan helps you navigate those choices, reach your goals, and protect yourself from unexpected situations. In this project, you'll create a comprehensive financial plan designed to address a specific real-world scenario.

Step 1: Choose Your Scenario

Select ONE of the scenarios below. They present different life stages and financial situations.

- **Scenario 1: The New Graduate**
    - You've just landed your first full-time job after college. You have some student loan debt, and you're eager to start saving for a car and eventually your own place.
- Job: Entry-level marketing coordinator in a mid-sized city.
- Salary: $42,000 per year (research average starting salaries in your area to adjust this if needed)
- Student Loans: $25,000 in federal loans, standard 10-year repayment plan.
    - You can use an online loan calculator to estimate the monthly payment amount based on current interest rates.
- Living Situation: Renting a room in a shared apartment to save money.
- Goals:
    - Pay down student loans as quickly as possible.
    - Save $5,000 for a reliable used car within a year.
    - Start contributing to a retirement account (even a small amount).
- Location: Mid-sized city (like Roanoke)
- Transportation: Relies on a combination of public transportation and occasional ridesharing for now. Eventually owning a car is the goal.
- Other Considerations: Desires some budget flexibility for social activities and travel back home to visit family a few times a year.

- **Scenario 2: The Balancing Act**
    - You're a parent of a young child, returning to work after taking time off. Your partner has a job, but their income can sometimes be unpredictable. Together, you must budget for childcare, household costs, and start building an emergency fund.
- Jobs:
    - Parent 1: Returning to a previous office job, part-time (3 days a week) to start. Potential to expand to full-time within a year.
    - Parent 2: Freelance graphic designer, income fluctuates throughout the year. Averages $3,000 per month, but some months are much slower.
- Childcare: Need daycare 3 days a week for a toddler. Research typical daycare costs for your area.
- Housing: Currently renting a small apartment. Hoping to eventually buy a house but need significant savings for a down payment.
- Goals:
    - Establish an emergency fund of at least $3,000.
    - Start saving consistently for a house down payment.
    - Explore retirement savings options, even if only contributing small amounts initially.
- Location: Suburb located outside a major city (higher childcare costs, but generally lower rent than in the city center).
- Transportation: The family owns one older car. Parent 2 uses it a few days a week for client meetings.
- Other Considerations: Parent 2's freelance income means occasionally paying estimated quarterly taxes to avoid penalties. They also may need to invest in business-related expenses (software, etc.)

Step 2: Build Your Plan

Your financial plan should be well structured and detailed. Include the following components:

- **Income Analysis:**
    - List ALL sources of income (salary, freelance gigs, child support, etc.).
    - Calculate your net income (after taxes/deductions).

- **Detailed Budget:**
    - Organize your spending into categories relevant to your scenario. BE SPECIFIC! (housing, transportation, groceries, entertainment, student loans, childcare, etc.)
    - Use realistic numbers. Do some online research to estimate typical costs in your area.

- **Savings & Debt Management:**
    - Establish a savings goal. How much can you realistically set aside each month? How will this help you achieve short-term (a car) and long-term (down-payment on a house) goals?
    - If you have debt, outline a payment plan that balances paying it off with reaching your other goals.
- **Investing for the Future:**
    - If your scenario allows for it, research suitable investment options (retirement account, a simple stock portfolio). Even starting small gets you in the investment habit. Briefly explain your choices.
- **The Power of Budgeting:**
    - How can you adjust your budget to free up money for saving?

Step 3: Beyond the Numbers

- **Reflection & Concepts:** Write a few paragraphs addressing:
    - Which economic and personal finance concepts learned in our unit were most important for creating your plan? Explain how.
    - Did anything surprise you during this process about creating a financial plan?

How Your Plan Will Be Assessed

- **Thoroughness & Accuracy:** Did you cover all components and calculate realistically?
- **Concept Application:** Do your choices demonstrate an understanding of budgeting, saving, debt management, and investing (if applicable)?
- **Justification:** Can you explain the reasoning behind your budgeting decisions and savings/investment choices?

Tips

- **Be Creative:** You can use spreadsheets, word processing, or even more visual formats to present your plan!
- **Resources:** Use reputable websites on personal finance for support and realistic data. [Include some trusted website suggestions if you have them]
- **Ask Questions:** Don't hesitate to ask for clarification or guidance throughout the project.

Day 12 Lesson Plan: Gamification & Your Future Finances

Objectives:

- Students will reflect on the gamified learning experiences and their insights into economic and personal finance principles.
- Students will identify practical takeaways
- from the unit and make commitments to improve their own financial decision-making.

Materials:

- Whiteboard or chart paper
- Markers
- "Personal Finance Pledge" worksheet (see below for a simple template)

Procedure

1. **Warm-up: Game Favorites & What Stuck (10 minutes)**
   - Quick poll: Which game from the unit was their favorite? Why?
   - For each game briefly revisit: What key concept(s) was that game meant to illustrate? (scarcity, budgeting, market forces, etc.)

2. **Reflection on Gamification (20 minutes)**
   - Questions for discussion or a written reflection:
     - How did using games as part of learning compare to other learning methods (lectures, worksheets, etc.)?
     - Did the games make economic and personal finance concepts easier to understand? Explain.
     - Were there any aspects of the games that were confusing or could be improved?
   - Summarize on the board: Pros and Cons of Gamification (based on student feedback)

3. **From Games to Real Life (15 minutes)**
   - Shift the focus: "We used simplified scenarios within the games. Let's talk about how this all connects to your future..."
   - Brainstorm as a class: List out 5-6 common financial decisions students will likely face soon (renting an apartment, managing credit, buying a car, etc.)
   - Ask: Which unit concepts are MOST important to be mindful of when making these real-life choices?

4. **Personal Finance Pledge Activity (15-20 minutes)**

- Distribute the "Personal Finance Pledge" worksheet.
- Students spend time individually making specific, actionable pledges relating to what they've learned.
- Optional: Allow a few minutes for students to share their pledges with a partner or in small groups for additional inspiration.

5. **Unit Wrap-Up (5 minutes)**
    - Emphasize that their financial journey is just beginning, and learning good habits now will have a ripple effect.
    - Leave them with a motivational prompt: "What's one small positive financial decision you will make this week?"

Handout T

Gamification Reflection Worksheet

Name:

Our Unit Games: List the 2-3 main games (The Price is Right, Plinko Budgeting, etc.) we played as a class:

Answer Honestly:

- Compared to studying using just textbook readings or regular worksheets, learning through games was...

(Circle one):

    More Engaging   About the Same   Less Engaging

- Did the games make the concepts we were learning easier, harder, or about the same difficulty to understand? Explain your answer:

- Think about your favorite game from the unit. Why did you like it? (Was it the competition, the story, the chance element, etc.)?

Beyond the Fun:

- Name ONE concept (like inflation, budgeting, opportunity cost) you understand more clearly now BECAUSE of a specific game we played. Explain how the game helped you understand.

- Did any of the games make you realize an area of personal finance (saving, budgeting, etc.) where you might want to make changes in your own life? Describe.

Your Honest Opinion:

- Would you want more game-based learning in other classes? Why or why not?

- What's one way a game from our unit could be made even better for learning?

The Price is Econ Completion Award

THIS PAGE LEFT INTENTIONALLY BLANK

THE PRICE IS ECON WINNER!

Presented to: _____

Demonstrated an understanding of Economic and Personal Finance Topics while a contestant on the Price is Econ and is now better prepared to make solid financial decisions in the future!

Jeremiah Riesenbeck
Jeremiah Riesenbeck
Producer of the Price is Economics

_____
Host

Made in the USA
Columbia, SC
23 September 2024